# FUNDAMENTALS OF WINDOWS REGISTRY

## BY

**DR BIENVENUE MAULA**

## What is an Operating System?

An **Operating System (OS)** is a software that acts as an interface between computer hardware components and the user. Every computer system must have at least one operating system to run other programs. Applications like Browsers, MS Office, Notepad Games, etc., need some environment to run and perform its tasks.

The OS helps you to communicate with the computer without knowing how to speak the computer's language. It is not possible for the user to use any computer or mobile device without having an operating system.

**HARDWARE**
• CPU, Memory, Hard Drive

**OPERATING SYSTEM**
• Windows, Apple OS X, Linux

**END USER**

Introduction to Operating System

The Windows Registry is a directory that stores settings and options for the operating system for Microsoft Windows. It contains information and settings for all the hardware, operating system software, most non-operating system software, users, preferences of the PC, etc.

This post talks about Windows Registry Basics.

- The registry is a database file or presentation that is used by all windows operating systems that followed Win95.
- The registry is used by the Windows OS to store hardware and software configuration information, user preferences and setup information.
- The correct registry is essential for correct windows performance and functioning, this is why the registry is usually attacked by viruses and other malicious software.

The Windows registry was introduced to tidy up the profusion of per-program INI files that had previously been used to store configuration settings for Windows programs. These files tended to be scattered all over the system, which made them difficult to track.

## History Of OS

- Operating systems were first developed in the late 1950s to manage tape storage
- The General Motors Research Lab implemented the first OS in the early 1950s for their IBM 701
- In the mid-1960s, operating systems started to use disks
- In the late 1960s, the first version of the Unix OS was developed
- The first OS built by Microsoft was DOS. It was built in 1981 by purchasing the 86-DOS

Whenever a user makes changes to Control Panel settings, file associations, system policies, or most installed software, the changes are reflected and stored in the registry. The registry also provides a window into the operation of the kernel, exposing runtime information such as performance counters and currently active hardware.

software from a Seattle company

- The present-day popular OS Windows first came to existence in 1985 when a GUI was created and paired with MS-DOS.

# Examples of Operating System with Market Share

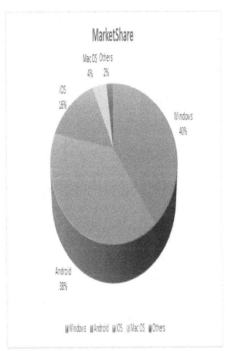

Market Share of Operating Systems

Following are the Operating System examples with the latest Market Share

| OS Name | Share |
| --- | --- |
| Windows | 40.34 |
| Android | 37.95 |
| iOS | 15.44 |
| Mac OS | 4.34 |
| Linux | 0.95 |
| Chrome OS | 0.14 |
| Windows Phone OS | 0.06 |

# Types of Operating System (OS)

Following are the popular types of OS (Operating System):

- Batch Operating System
- Multitasking/Time Sharing OS
- Multiprocessing OS
- Real Time OS
- Distributed OS

- Network OS
- Mobile OS

## Batch Operating System

Some computer processes are very lengthy and time-consuming. To speed the same process, a job with a similar type of needs are batched together and run as a group.

The user of a batch operating system never directly interacts with the computer. In this type of OS, every user prepares his or her job on an offline device like a punch card and submit it to the computer operator.

## Multi-Tasking/Time-sharing Operating systems

Time-sharing operating system enables people located at a different terminal(shell) to use a single computer system at the same time. The processor time (CPU) which is shared among multiple users is termed as time sharing.

## Real time OS

A real time operating system time interval to process and respond to inputs is very small. Examples: Military Software Systems, Space Software Systems are the Real time OS example.

## Distributed Operating System

Distributed systems use many processors located in different machines to provide very fast computation to its users.

**Network Operating System**

Network Operating System runs on a server. It provides the capability to serve to manage data, user, groups, security, application, and other networking functions.

**Mobile OS**

Mobile operating systems are those OS which is especially that are designed to power smartphones, tablets, and wearables devices.

Some most famous mobile operating systems are Android and iOS, but others include BlackBerry, Web, and watchOS.

# Functions of Operating System

Some typical operating system functions may include managing memory, files, processes, I/O system & devices, security, etc.

Below are the main functions of Operating System:

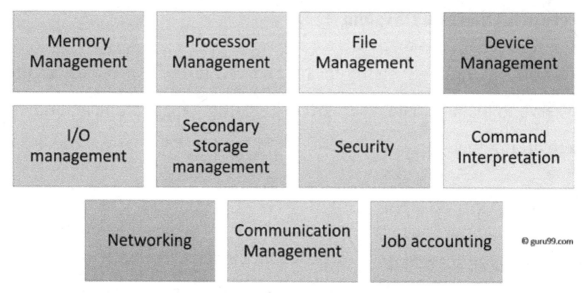

Functions of Operating System

In an operating system software performs each of the function:

1. **Process management**: Process management helps OS to create and delete processes. It also provides mechanisms for synchronization and communication among processes.

2. **Memory management:** Memory management module performs the task of allocation and de-allocation of memory space to programs in need of this resources.

3. **File management**: It manages all the file-related activities such as organization storage, retrieval, naming, sharing, and protection of files.

4. **Device Management**: Device management keeps tracks of all devices. This module also responsible for this task is known as the I/O controller. It also performs the task of allocation and de-allocation of the devices.

5. **I/O System Management:** One of the main objects of any OS is to hide the peculiarities of that hardware devices from the user.

6. **Secondary-Storage Management**: Systems have several levels of storage which includes primary storage, secondary storage, and cache storage. Instructions and data must be stored in primary storage or cache so that a running program can reference it.

7. **Security**: Security module protects the data and information of a computer system against malware threat and authorized access.

8. **Command interpretation**: This module is interpreting commands given by the and acting system resources to process that commands.

9. **Networking:** A distributed system is a group of processors which do not share memory, hardware devices, or a clock. The processors communicate with one another through the network.

10. **Job accounting**: Keeping track of time & resource used by various job and users.

11. **Communication management**: Coordination and assignment of compilers, interpreters, and another software resource of the various users of the computer systems.

# Features of Operating System (OS)

Here is a list important features of OS:

- Protected and supervisor mode
- Allows disk access and file systems Device drivers Networking Security
- Program Execution
- Memory management Virtual Memory Multitasking

- Handling I/O operations

- Manipulation of the file system

- Error Detection and handling

- Resource allocation

- Information and Resource Protection

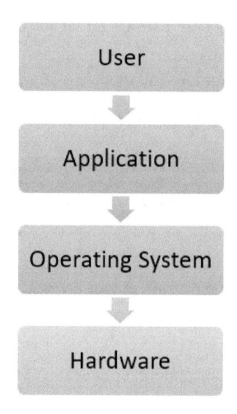

# **Advantage of Operating System**

- Allows you to hide details of hardware by creating an abstraction

- Easy to use with a GUI

- Offers an environment in which a user may execute programs/applications

- The operating system must make sure that the computer system convenient to use

- Operating System acts as an intermediary among applications and the hardware components
- It provides the computer system resources with easy to use format
- Acts as an intermediator between all hardware's and software's of the system

# Disadvantages of Operating System

- If any issue occurs in OS, you may lose all the contents which have been stored in your system
- Operating system's software is quite expensive for small size organization which adds burden on them. Example Windows
- It is never entirely secure as a threat can occur at any time

# What is Kernel in Operating System?

The kernel is the central component of a computer operating systems. The only job performed by the kernel is to the manage the communication between the software and the hardware. A Kernel is at the nucleus of a computer. It makes the communication between the hardware and software possible. While the Kernel is the innermost part of an operating system, a shell is the outermost one.

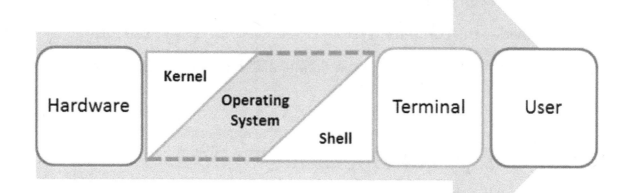

Introduction to Kernel

# Features of Kernel

- Low-level scheduling of processes
- Inter-process communication
- Process synchronization
- Context switching

# Types of Kernel

There are many types of kernels that exists, but among them, the two most popular kernels are:

## 1. Monolithic

A monolithic kernel is a single code or block of the program. It provides all the required services offered by the operating system. It is a simplistic design which creates a distinct communication layer between the hardware and software.

## 2. Microkernels

Microkernel manages all system resources. In this type of kernel, services are implemented in different address space. The user services are stored in user address space, and kernel services are stored under kernel address space. So, it helps to reduce the size of both the kernel and operating system.

# Difference between Firmware and Operating System

Below are the Key Differences between Firmware and Operating System:

| Firmware | Operating System |
|---|---|
| Define Firmware: Firmware is one kind of programming that is embedded on a chip in the device which controls that specific device. | Define Operating System: OS provides functionality over and above that which is provided by the firmware. |
| Firmware is programs that been encoded by the manufacture of the IC or something and cannot be changed. | OS is a program that can be installed by the user and can be changed. |

| | |
|---|---|
| It is stored on non-volatile memory. | OS is stored on the hard drive. |

# Difference between 32-Bit and 64-Bit Operating System

Below are the Key Differences between 32-Bit and 64-Bit Operating System:

| Parameters | 32. Bit | 64. Bit |
|---|---|---|
| Architecture and Software | Allow 32 bit of data processing simultaneously | Allow 64 bit of data processing simultaneously |
| Compatibility | 32-bit applications require 32-bit OS and CPUs. | 64-bit applications require a 64-bit OS and CPU. |
| Systems Available | All versions of Windows 8, Windows 7, Windows Vista, and Windows XP, Linux, etc. | Windows XP Professional, Vista, 7, Mac OS X and Linux. |
| Memory Limits | 32-bit systems are limited to 3.2 GB of RAM. | 64-bit systems allow a maximum 17 Billion GB of RAM. |

# Registry Editor

Over the years we've covered a lot of registry hacks, and while most people can handle the step-by-step instructions for how to make a registry change, or double-click a .reg file to insert it into the registry, you will be much better served having a solid knowledge of what the registry is and how it works.

The most important thing to know about the registry is that you probably shouldn't just mess around and delete or change things for no reason. Deleting a big portion of the registry is never going to make your computer run faster, and there's no registry hack that will speed up your computer or give you some major new functionality that doesn't exist.

Almost all registry hacks involve either tweaking the behavior of some component in Windows, or disabling a behavior that you don't like. For instance, if you want to disable SkyDrive / OneDrive from Windows entirely, you can use a registry hack to accomplish it. If you are tired of Windows Update forcibly rebooting your computer, you can hack the registry to make it stop.

The **Windows Registry** is a directory that stores settings and options for the operating system for Microsoft Windows. It contains information and settings for all the hardware, operating system software, most non-operating system software, users, preferences of the PC, etc. This post talks about **Windows Registry Basics**.

Microsoft definition:

"...a central hierarchical database used ... to store information that is necessary to configure the system for one or more users, applications and hardware devices."

Whenever a user makes changes to Control Panel settings, file associations, system policies, or most installed software, the changes are reflected and stored in the registry. The registry also provides a window into the operation of the kernel, exposing runtime information such as performance counters and currently active hardware.

The Windows registry was introduced to tidy up the profusion of per-program INI files that had previously been used to store configuration settings for Windows programs. These files tended to be scattered all over the system, which made them difficult to track.

Click **Start** or press the Windows key . In the Start menu, either in the Run box or the Search box, type regedit and press Enter . In Windows 8, you can type regedit on the Start screen and select the regedit option in the search results. In Windows 10, type regedit in the Search box on the taskbar and press Enter

# Windows Registry Basics

**The Registry consists of the following 5 Root Keys**:

- HKEY_CLASSES_ROOT
- HKEY_CURRENT_USER
- HKEY_LOCAL_MACHINE
- HKEY_USERS
- HKEY_CURRENT_CONFIG.

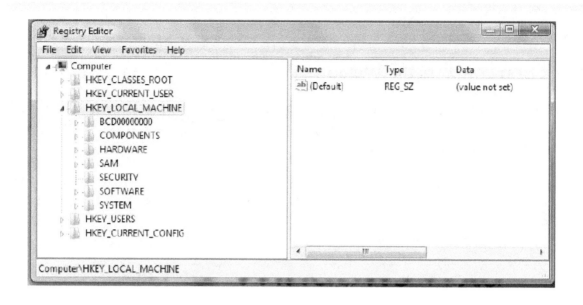

Root Keys contain **SubKeys**. *Subkeys may contain subkeys of their own too and contain at least one value, called as its* **Default Value**. A key with all its subkeys and values is called as a **Hive**.

The Registry is located on the Disk in the system32/config folder as several separate Hive files. These Hive files are then read into memory every time Windows starts or when the User logs on. To see where the Hives are physically stored, see:

`HKEY_LOCAL_MACHINE\System\CurrentControlSet\Control\HiveList`

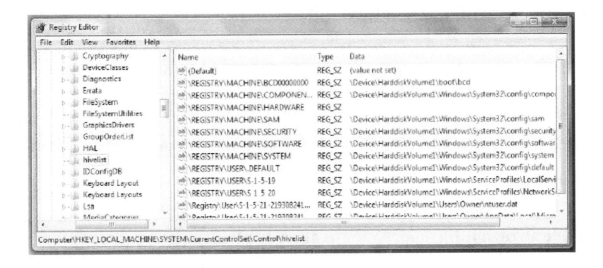

You can read more about the location of Windows Registry files.

**The Registry uses the following data types:**

- **REG_SZ** : The SZ indicates a zero-terminated string. This is a variable-length string that can contain Unicode as well as ANSI characters.

- **REG_BINARY** : It contains binary data. 0's & 1's.

- **REG_DWORD** : This data type is a Double Word. It is a 32-bit numeric value and can hold any number from 0 to 232.

- **REG_QWORD** : This data type is a Quadruple Word. It is a 64-bit numeric value.

- **REG_MULTI_SZ** : This data type contains a group of zero-terminated strings assigned to a single value.

- **REG_EXPAND_SZ** : This data type is a zero-terminated string containing an unexpanded reference to an environment variable, like say, %SystemRoot%.

## Registry Virtualization in Windows

Starting with Windows Vista, along with File Virtualization, the Registry too, has been Virtualized, and hence unlike Windows XP, does not tend to suffer from bloat. The same has been continued in Windows 7.

**Virtualization basically means that applications are prevented from writing to System Folders Windows' file system and ALSO to the '*machine wide keys*' in the registry. However, this does not prevent standard user accounts from installing or running applications.**

In Windows Vista and later, the UAC utilizes the Registry Virtualization Feature, to redirect attempts to write to subkeys of

```
HKEY_LOCAL_MACHINE\Software
```

When an application attempts to write to this hive, Vista instead, writes it, to a per-user location,

```
HKEY_CLASSES_ROOT\VirtualStore\Machine\Software
```

This is done discreetly. No one gets to know that this is happening!

*This is, in short, Registry Virtualization, and it is a useful Security feature.*

Incidentally, mention must also be made of another new technology underlying Windows Vista and later: The Kernel Transaction

Manager, which enables the Transactional Registry. This feature enables a sort of a Registry rollback. But it's not implemented in Registry Editor. Instead, this feature is designed for use by developers who need to create robust applications using transactional processing.

**Read:** How to create a Registry Key in Windows.

**Registry Editor**

The primary tool in Windows 10/8/7/Vista for working directly with the registry is **Registry Editor**. To access it, simply type *regedit* in Vista's Start Menu Search Bar and hit Enter!

You have to be doubly careful when working with the Registry, as there is no confirmation prompt or a click OK to save prompt. Changes made are directly incorporated.

You can read more about Windows Registry Editor Tips & Features. Users of Windows 10 v1703 can use the Address Bar to jump directly to any registry key.

Mention must specifically be made of the

```
HKEY_LOCAL_MACHINE\System\CurrentControlSet
```

hive as the keys in this particular is so essential for Windows to start-up, that its backup is maintained, which you can restore when necessary, simply by booting in Safe Mode and selecting *Last Known Good Configuration*

## What is the Registry?

The Windows Registry is a hierarchical database that contains all of the configurations and settings used by components, services, applications, and pretty much everything in Windows.

ADVERTISEMENT

The registry has two basic concepts to be aware of: Keys and Values. Registry Keys are objects that are basically folders, and in the interface even look exactly like folders. Values are a bit like the files in the folders, and they contain the actual settings.

When you open the Registry Editor for the first time, you'll see a treeview on the left-hand pane that contains all of the keys, with values on the right-hand side. It's about as simple as an interface gets.

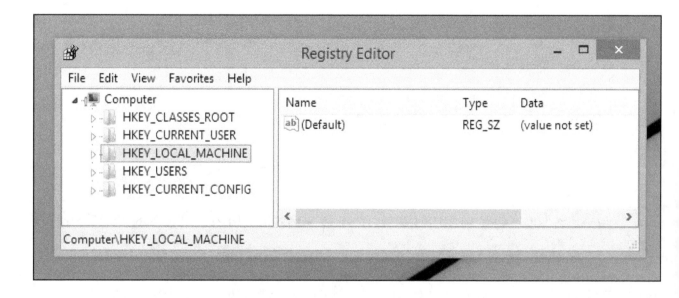

The root-level keys that you see in the left-hand side of the screenshot are important. Each one houses a different set of information, so depending on what you are trying to do, you'll need to know which section to browse down into.

The interesting thing that most people don't know is that three of the five items on the root level aren't actually there… they are just linked to items further down in one of the other keys.

### HKEY_CLASSES_ROOT

Windows uses this section to manage file type associations, and it is usually abbreviated HKCR when being referenced in documentation. This key is actually just a link to HKLM\Software\Classes.

You can also use this section if you want to tweak the context menu for a particular file type.

### HKEY_CURRENT_USER

Holds the user settings for the currently logged in user, and is usually abbreviated HKCU This is actually just a link to HKEY_USERS\<SID-FOR-CURRENT-USER>. The most important sub-key in here is HKCU\Software, which contains user-level settings for most of your software.

*HKEY_LOCAL_MACHINE*

All of the system-wide settings are stored here, and it is usually abbreviated as HKLM. You'll mostly use the HKLM\Software key to check machine-wide settings.

*HKEY_USERS*

Stores all of the settings for all users on the system. You'll typically use HKCU instead, but if you need to check settings for another user on your computer, you can use this one.

*HKEY_CURRENT_CONFIG*

Stores all of the information about the current hardware configuration. This one isn't used very often, and it just a link to HKLM\SYSTEM\CurrentControlSet\Hardware Profiles\Current.

**Creating New Keys and Values**

Right-clicking on any key in the left-hand side of the window will give you a set of options, most of which are fairly straightforward and easy to understand.

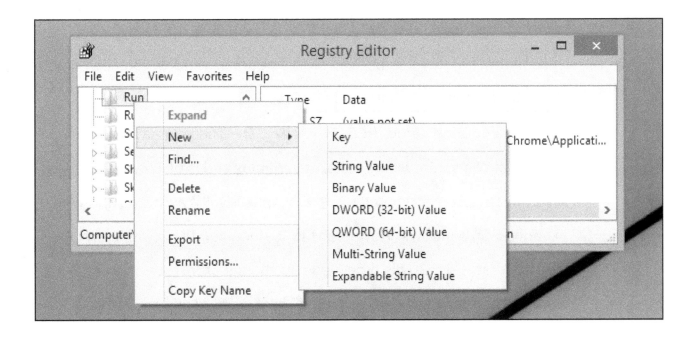

You can create a new Key, which will show up as a folder on the left-hand side, or a new value, which will show up on the right-hand side. Those values can be a little confusing, but there are really only a couple of values that are used regularly.

- **String Value (REG_SZ)** – This contains anything that will fit into a regular string. The vast majority of the time, you can edit human-readable strings without breaking everything.

- **Binary Value (REG_BINARY)** – This value contains arbitrary binary data, and you will almost never want to attempt to edit one of these keys.

- **DWORD (32-bit) Value (REG_DWORD)** – These are almost always used for a regular integer value, whether just 0 or 1, or a number from 0 to 4,294,967,295.

- **QWORD (64-bit) Value (REG_QWORD)** – These are not used very often for registry hacking purposes, but it's basically a 64-bit integer value.

- **Multi-String Value (REG_MULTI_SZ)** – These values are fairly uncommon, but it works basically like a notepad window. You can type multi-line textual information into a field like this.

- **Expandable String Value (REG_EXPAND_SZ)** – These variables have a string that can contain environment variables and is often used for system paths. So a string might be %SystemDrive%\Windows and would expand to C:\Windows. This means that when you find a value in the Registry that is set to this type, you can change or insert environment variables and they will be "expanded" before the string is used.

Fun Fact: DWORD is short for "Double Word," because a "Word" is a term for the default unit of data used by a processor, and when Windows was created that was 16 bits. So a "word" is 16 bits, and a "Double Word" is 32 bits. While modern processors are all 64-bit, the Registry still uses the older format for compatibility.

## The Favorites Menu

One of the really useful features that nobody seems to notice is the Favorites menu, which is great when you want to check a registry location regularly. What's really fun is that you can export the list of favorites and use it again on another computer without having to browse down to the keys and add them to the favorites menu.

It's also a great way to bookmark something in the registry if you are looking around in multiple locations, so you can easily flip back to the last place you were at.

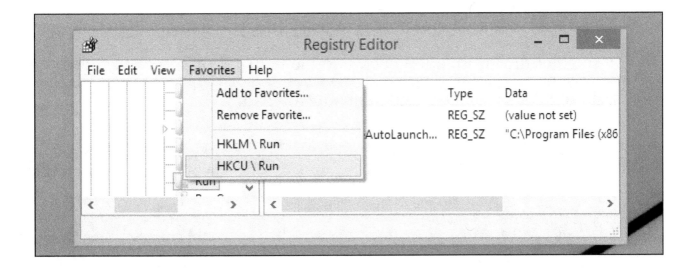

## Exporting Registry Files

You can export registry keys and all of the values contained underneath them by right-clicking on a key and choosing Export. This is really important if you are going to be making changes to your system.

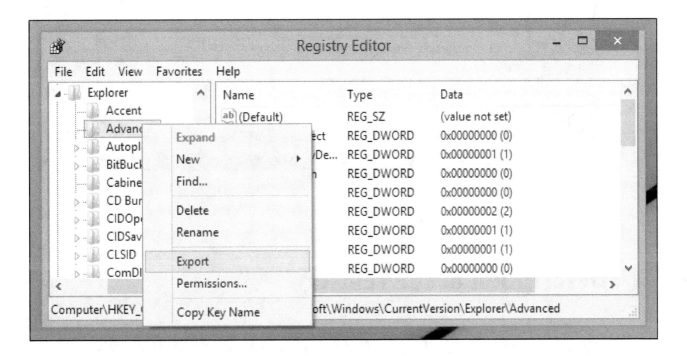

Once you've got your exported registry file, you can double-click on it to enter the information back into the registry, or you can choose Edit to take a look at the contents in Notepad.

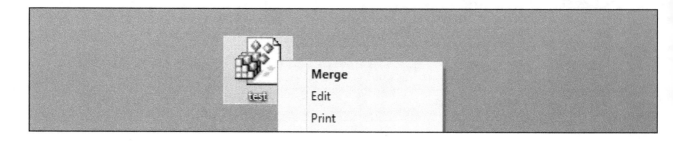

The registry hacking file format is pretty simple – value names on the left, and actual values on the right.

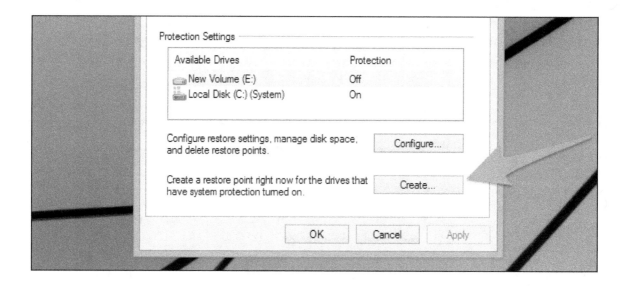

# Description of the registry

The *Microsoft Computer Dictionary*, Fifth Edition, defines the registry as:

A central hierarchical database used in Windows 98, Windows CE, Windows NT, and Windows 2000 used to store information that is necessary to configure the system for one or more users, applications, and hardware devices.

The Registry contains information that Windows continually references during operation, such as profiles for each user, the applications installed on the computer and the types of documents that each can create, property sheet settings for folders and application icons, what hardware exists on the system, and the ports that are being used.

The Registry replaces most of the text-based .ini files that are used in Windows 3.x and MS-DOS configuration files, such as the Autoexec.bat and Config.sys. Although the Registry is common to several Windows operating systems, there are some differences among them. A registry hive is a group of keys, subkeys, and values in the registry that has a set of supporting files that contain backups of its data. The supporting files for all hives except HKEY_CURRENT_USER are in the %SystemRoot%\System32\Config folder on Windows NT 4.0, Windows 2000, Windows XP, Windows Server 2003, and Windows Vista. The supporting files for HKEY_CURRENT_USER are in the %SystemRoot%\Profiles\Username folder. The file name extensions of the files in these folders indicate the type of data that they contain.

Also, the lack of an extension may sometimes indicate the type of data that they contain.

| Description of the registry | |
|---|---|
| **Registry hive** | **Supporting files** |
| HKEY_LOCAL_MACHINE\SAM | Sam, Sam.log, Sam.sav |
| HKEY_LOCAL_MACHINE\Security | Security, Security.log, Security.sav |
| HKEY_LOCAL_MACHINE\Software | Software, Software.log, Software.sav |
| HKEY_LOCAL_MACHINE\System | System, System.alt, System.log, System.sav |
| HKEY_CURRENT_CONFIG | System, System.alt, System.log, System.sav, Ntuser.dat, Ntuser.dat.log |
| HKEY_USERS\DEFAULT | Default, Default.log, Default.sav |

In Windows 98, the registry files are named User.dat and System.dat. In Windows Millennium Edition, the registry files are named Classes.dat, User.dat, and System.dat.

Note

Security features in Windows let an administrator control access to registry keys.

The following table lists the predefined keys that are used by the system. The maximum size of a key name is 255 characters.

| Table 2 | |
|---|---|
| **Folder/predefined key** | **Description** |
| HKEY_CURRENT_USER | Contains the root of the configuration information for the user who is currently logged on. The user's folders, screen colors, and Control Panel settings are stored here. This information is associated with the user's profile. This key is sometimes abbreviated as *HKCU*. |
| HKEY_USERS | Contains all the actively loaded user profiles on the computer. HKEY_CURRENT_USER is a subkey of HKEY_USERS. HKEY_USERS is sometimes abbreviated as *HKU*. |
| HKEY_LOCAL_MACHINE | Contains configuration information particular to the computer (for any user). This key is sometimes abbreviated as *HKLM*. |
| HKEY_CLASSES_ROOT | Is a subkey of `HKEY_LOCAL_MACHINE\Software`. The |

| Table 2 | |
|---|---|
| **Folder/predefined key** | **Description** |
| | information that is stored here makes sure that the correct program opens when you open a file by using Windows Explorer. This key is sometimes abbreviated as *HKCR*. Starting with Windows 2000, this information is stored under both the HKEY_LOCAL_MACHINE and HKEY_CURRENT_USER keys. The `HKEY_LOCAL_MACHINE\Software\Classes` key contains default settings that can apply to all users on the local computer. The `HKEY_CURRENT_USER\Software\Classes` key contains settings that override the default settings and apply only to the interactive user. The HKEY_CLASSES_ROOT key provides a view of the registry that merges the information from these two sources. HKEY_CLASSES_ROOT also provides this merged view for programs that are designed for earlier |

| Folder/predefined key | Description |
|---|---|
| | versions of Windows. To change the settings for the interactive user, changes must be made under `HKEY_CURRENT_USER\Software\Classes` instead of under HKEY_CLASSES_ROOT. To change the default settings, changes must be made under `HKEY_LOCAL_MACHINE\Software\Classes`. If you write keys to a key under HKEY_CLASSES_ROOT, the system stores the information under `HKEY_LOCAL_MACHINE\Software\Classes`. If you write values to a key under HKEY_CLASSES_ROOT, and the key already exists under `HKEY_CURRENT_USER\Software\Classes`, the system will store the information there instead of under `HKEY_LOCAL_MACHINE\Software\Classes`. |
| HKEY_CURRENT_CONFIG | Contains information about the hardware profile that is used by the |

| Table 2 | |
|---|---|
| **Folder/predefined key** | **Description** |
| | local computer at system startup. |

Note

The registry in 64-bit versions of Windows XP, Windows Server 2003, and Windows Vista is divided into 32-bit and 64-bit keys. Many of the 32-bit keys have the same names as their 64-bit counterparts, and vice versa. The default 64-bit version of Registry Editor that is included with 64-bit versions of Windows XP, Windows Server 2003, and Windows Vista displays the 32-bit keys under the node `HKEY_LOCAL_MACHINE\Software\WOW6432Node`. For more information about how to view the registry on 64-Bit versions of Windows, see How to view the system registry by using 64-bit versions of Windows.

The following table lists the data types that are currently defined and that are used by Windows. The maximum size of a value name is as follows:

- Windows Server 2003, Windows XP, and Windows Vista: 16,383 characters
- Windows 2000: 260 ANSI characters or 16,383 Unicode characters

- Windows Millennium Edition/Windows 98/Windows 95: 255 characters

Long values (more than 2,048 bytes) must be stored as files with the file names stored in the registry. This helps the registry perform efficiently. The maximum size of a value is as follows:

- Windows NT 4.0/Windows 2000/Windows XP/Windows Server 2003/Windows Vista: Available memory
- Windows Millennium Edition/Windows 98/Windows 95: 16,300 bytes

Note

There is a 64K limit for the total size of all values of a key.

| Table 3 | | |
|---------|---|---|
| **Name** | **Data type** | **Description** |
| Binary Value | REG_BINARY | Raw binary data. Most hardware component information is stored as binary data and is displayed in Registry Editor in hexadecimal format. |
| DWOR D Value | REG_DWORD | Data represented by a number that is 4 bytes |

| Table 3 | | |
|---|---|---|
| **Name** | **Data type** | **Description** |
| | | long (a 32-bit integer). Many parameters for device drivers and services are this type and are displayed in Registry Editor in binary, hexadecimal, or decimal format. Related values are DWORD_LITTLE_EN DIAN (least significant byte is at the lowest address) and REG_DWORD_BIG_E NDIAN (least significant byte is at the highest address). |
| Expanda ble String Value | REG_EXPAND_SZ | A variable-length data string. This data type includes variables that are resolved when a program or service uses |

| Name | Data type | Description |
|---|---|---|
| | | the data. |
| Multi-String Value | REG_MULTI_SZ | A multiple string. Values that contain lists or multiple values in a form that people can read are generally this type. Entries are separated by spaces, commas, or other marks. |
| String Value | REG_SZ | A fixed-length text string. |
| Binary Value | REG_RESOURCE_LIST | A series of nested arrays that is designed to store a resource list that is used by a hardware device driver or one of the physical devices it controls. This data is detected and written in the \ResourceMap tree by the system and is |

Table 3

| Table 3 | | |
|---|---|---|
| **Name** | **Data type** | **Description** |
| | | displayed in Registry Editor in hexadecimal format as a Binary Value. |
| Binary Value | REG_RESOURCE_REQUIREME NTS_LIST | A series of nested arrays that is designed to store a device driver's list of possible hardware resources the driver or one of the physical devices it controls can use. The system writes a subset of this list in the \ResourceMap tree. This data is detected by the system and is displayed in Registry Editor in hexadecimal format as a Binary Value. |
| Binary Value | REG_FULL_RESOURCE_DESC RIPTOR | A series of nested arrays that is designed to store |

| Name | Data type | Description |
|------|-----------|-------------|
|  |  | a resource list that is used by a physical hardware device. This data is detected and written in the \HardwareDescription tree by the system and is displayed in Registry Editor in hexadecimal format as a Binary Value. |
| None | REG_NONE | Data without any particular type. This data is written to the registry by the system or applications and is displayed in Registry Editor in hexadecimal format as a Binary Value |
| Link | REG_LINK | A Unicode string naming a symbolic link. |

Table 3

| Table 3 | | |
|---|---|---|
| **Name** | **Data type** | **Description** |
| QWORD Value | REG_QWORD | Data represented by a number that is a 64-bit integer. This data is displayed in Registry Editor as a Binary Value and was introduced in Windows 2000. |

# Back up the registry

Before you edit the registry, export the keys in the registry that you plan to edit, or back up the whole registry. If a problem occurs, you can then follow the steps in the Restore the registry section to restore the registry to its previous state. To back up the whole registry, use the Backup utility to back up the system state. The system state includes the registry, the COM+ Class Registration Database, and your boot files. For more information about how to use the Backup utility to back up the system state, see the following articles:

- Back up and restore your PC
- How to use the backup feature to back up and restore data in Windows Server 2003

# Edit the registry

To modify registry data, a program must use the registry functions that are defined in <u>Registry Functions</u>.

Administrators can modify the registry by using Registry Editor (Regedit.exe or Regedt32.exe), Group Policy, System Policy, Registry (.reg) files, or by running scripts such as VisualBasic script files.

**Use the Windows user interface**

We recommend that you use the Windows user interface to change your system settings instead of manually editing the registry. However, editing the registry may sometimes be the best method to resolve a product issue. If the issue is documented in the Microsoft Knowledge Base, an article with step-by-step instructions to edit the registry for that issue will be available. We recommend that you follow those instructions exactly.

**Use Registry Editor**

Warning

Serious problems might occur if you modify the registry incorrectly by using Registry Editor or by using another method. These problems might require that you reinstall the operating system. Microsoft cannot guarantee that these problems can be solved. Modify the registry at your own risk.

You can use Registry Editor to do the following actions:

- Locate a subtree, key, subkey, or value
- Add a subkey or a value
- Change a value
- Delete a subkey or a value
- Rename a subkey or a value

The navigation area of Registry Editor displays folders. Each folder represents a predefined key on the local computer. When you access the registry of a remote computer, only two predefined keys appear: HKEY_USERS and HKEY_LOCAL_MACHINE.

**Use Group Policy**

Microsoft Management Console (MMC) hosts administrative tools that you can use to administer networks, computers, services, and other system components. The Group Policy MMC snap-in lets administrators define policy settings that are applied to computers or users. You can implement Group Policy on local computers by using the local Group Policy MMC snap-in, Gpedit.msc. You can implement Group Policy in Active Directory by using the Active Directory Users and Computers MMC snap-in. For more information about how to use Group Policy, see the Help topics in the appropriate Group Policy MMC snap-in.

## Use a Registration Entries (.reg) file

Create a Registration Entries (.reg) file that contains the registry changes, and then run the .reg file on the computer where you want to make the changes. You can run the .reg file manually or by using a logon script. For more information, see How to add, modify, or delete registry subkeys and values by using a Registration Entries (.reg) file.

## Use Windows Script Host

The Windows Script Host lets you run VBScript and JScript scripts directly in the operating system. You can create VBScript and JScript files that use Windows Script Host methods to delete, to read, and to write registry keys and values. For more information about these methods, visit the following Microsoft Web sites:

- RegDelete method
- RegRead method
- RegWrite method

## Use Windows Management Instrumentation

Windows Management Instrumentation (WMI) is a component of the Microsoft Windows operating system and is the Microsoft implementation of Web-Based Enterprise Management (WBEM). WBEM is an industry initiative to develop a standard technology for accessing management information in an enterprise environment. You can use WMI to automate administrative tasks (such as editing the registry) in an enterprise environment. You can use WMI in scripting languages that have an engine on Windows and that handle Microsoft ActiveX objects. You can also use the WMI Command-Line utility (Wmic.exe) to modify the Windows registry.

For more information about WMI, see Windows Management Instrumentation.

For more information about the WMI Command-Line utility, see A description of the Windows Management Instrumentation (WMI) command-line utility (Wmic.exe).

**Use Console Registry Tool for Windows**

You can use the Console Registry Tool for Windows (Reg.exe) to edit the registry. For help with the Reg.exe tool, type `reg /?` at the Command Prompt, and then click **OK**.

# Restore the registry

To restore the registry, use the appropriate method.

### Method 1: Restore the registry keys

To restore registry subkeys that you exported, double-click the Registration Entries (.reg) file that you saved in the Export registry subkeys section. Or, you can restore the whole registry from a backup. For more information about how to restore the whole registry, see the Method 2: Restore the whole registry section later in this article.

**Method 2: Restore the whole registry**

To restore the whole registry, restore the system state from a backup. For more information about how to restore the system state from a backup, see How to use Backup to protect data and restore files and folders on your computer in Windows XP and Windows Vista.

Note

Backing up the system state also creates updated copies of the registry files in the `%SystemRoot%\Repair` folder.

# Administrative Tools

Administrative Tools is the collective name for several advanced tools in Windows that are used mainly by system administrators.

It's available in Windows 10, Windows 8, Windows 7, Windows Vista, Windows XP, and Windows Server operating system. Windows 11 calls these tools Windows Tools.

Below is a list of programs you'll find in Administrative Tools, complete with summaries, which versions of Windows they appear in, and links to more details about the programs, if we have any.

## What Are Administrative Tools Used For?

The programs can be used to schedule a test of your computer's memory, manage advanced aspects of users and groups, format hard drives, configure Windows services, change how the operating system starts, and much, much more.

## How to Access Administrative Tools

Since it's a Control Panel applet, it can be accessed via Control Panel. To find it, first, open Control Panel and then choose **Administrative Tools**.

If you're having trouble finding the Administrative Tools applet, change the Control Panel view to something other than *Home* or *Category*, depending on your version of Windows. For example, in Windows 10 or 8, you'd change the "View by" option to **Large icons** or **Small icons**.

The tools available in Administrative Tools can also be accessed through the special GodMode folder, but that's only useful if you've already enabled GodMode.

## How to Use Administrative Tools

This suite of tools is basically a folder that contains shortcuts to other parts of Windows where the tools are actually located. Double-clicking or double-tapping one of these shortcuts will start that tool.

In other words, Administrative Tools itself doesn't *do* anything. It is just a location that stores shortcuts to related programs that are actually stored in the *Windows* folder.

Most of the available programs are snap-ins for the Microsoft Management Console (MMC).

# Component Services

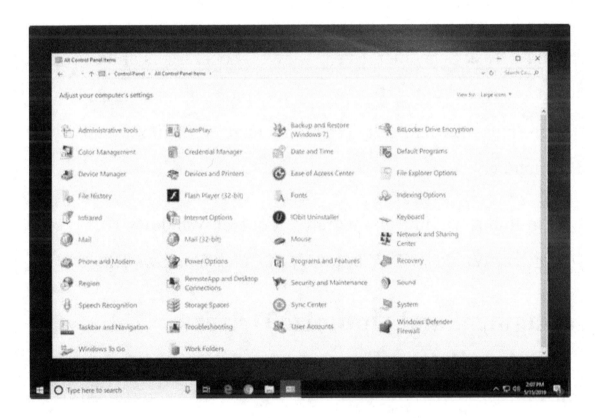

Component Services is an MMC snap-in used to administer and configure COM components, COM+ applications, and more.

It's included within Administrative Tools in Windows 10, Windows 8, Windows 7, and Windows XP. This tool does exist in Windows Vista (execute **comexp.msc** to start it) but for some reason wasn't included within Administrative Tools in that version of Windows.

# Computer Management

Computer Management is an MMC snap-in used as a central location to manage local or remote computers.

It includes Task Scheduler, Event Viewer, Local Users and Groups, Device Manager, Disk Management, and more, all in a single location. This makes it really easy to manage all the important aspects of a computer.

You can find it within Administrative Tools in Windows 10, Windows 8, Windows 7, Windows Vista, and Windows XP.

# Defragment and Optimize Drives

Defragment and Optimize Drives opens Microsoft Drive Optimizer, the built-in defragmentation tool in Windows.

It's included within Administrative Tools in Windows 10 and Windows 8. Windows 7, Windows Vista, and Windows XP all have defragmentation tools included but they're not available via Administrative Tools in those versions of Windows.

Other companies make defrag software that competes with Microsoft's built-in tools. See our list of free defrag software for some of the better ones.

## Disk Cleanup

Disk Cleanup opens Disk Space Cleanup Manager, a tool used to gain free disk space by removing unnecessary files like setup logs, temporary files, Windows Update caches, and more.

It's part of Administrative Tools in Windows 10 and Windows 8. You can also find it in Windows 7, Windows Vista, and Windows XP, but the tool isn't available via Administrative Tools.

A number of "cleaner" tools are available from companies other than Microsoft that do a lot more than what Disk Cleanup does. CCleaner is one of our favorites but there are other free PC cleaner tools out there, too.

## Event Viewer

Event Viewer is an MMC snap-in used to view information about certain actions in Windows, called *events*.

It can sometimes be used to identify a problem that has occurred in Windows, especially when an issue has occurred but no clear error message was received.

Events are stored in event logs. A number of Windows event logs exist, including Application, Security, System, Setup, and Forwarded Events.

Application specific and custom event logs exist in Event Viewer as well, logging events that occur with and are specific to certain programs.

This is included within Administrative Tools in Windows 10, Windows 8, Windows 7, Windows Vista, and Windows XP.

How to Use Event Viewer in Windows 10

# iSCSI Initiator

The iSCSI Initiator link in Administrative Tools starts the iSCSI Initiator Configuration Tool.

This program is used to manage the communication between networked iSCSI storage devices.

Since iSCSI devices are typically found in an enterprise or large business environments, you typically only see the iSCSI Initiator tool used with Server versions of Windows.

It's included within Administrative Tools in Windows 10, Windows 8, Windows 7, and Windows Vista.

# Local Security Policy

Local Security Policy is an MMC snap-in used to manage Group Policy security settings.

One example of using Local Security Policy would be requiring a minimum password length for user passwords, enforcing a maximum password age, or making sure any new password meets a certain level of complexity.

Pretty much any detailed restriction you can imagine can be set with Local Security Policy.

Local Security Policy is included within Administrative Tools in Windows 10, Windows 8, Windows 7, Windows Vista, and Windows XP.

# ODBC Data Sources

ODBC Data Sources (ODBC) opens ODBC Data Source Administrator, a program used to manage ODBC data sources.

ODBC Data Sources is included within Administrative Tools in Windows 10 and Windows 8.

If the version of Windows you're using is 64-bit, you'll see two versions, both an ODBC Data Sources (32-bit) and an ODBC Data Sources (64-bit) link, that are used to manage data sources for both 32-bit and 64-bit applications.

ODBC Data Source Administrator is accessible via Administrative Tools in Windows 7, Windows Vista, and Windows XP as well but the link is named **Data Sources (ODBC)**.

# Memory Diagnostics Tool

Memory Diagnostics Tool is the name of the shortcut in Administrative Tools in Windows Vista that starts Windows Memory Diagnostic on the next reboot.

This utility tests your computer's memory to identify defects, which may ultimately require you to replace your RAM.

It was renamed **Windows Memory Diagnostic** in later versions of Windows. You can read more about it near the end of this list.

# Performance Monitor

Performance Monitor is an MMC snap-in that's used to view real-time, or previously recorded, computer performance data.

Advanced information about your CPU, RAM, hard drive, and network are just a few of the things you can view via this tool.

Performance Monitor is included within Administrative Tools in Windows 10, Windows 8, and Windows 7.

In Windows Vista, the available functions are part of **Reliability and Performance Monitor**, available from Administrative Tools in that version of Windows.

In Windows XP, an older version of this tool, simply called **Performance**, is included in Administrative Tools.

# Print Management

Print Management is an MMC snap-in used as a central location to manage local and network printer settings, installed printer drivers, current print jobs, and much more.

Basic printer management is still best performed from **Devices and Printers** (Windows 10, 8, 7, and Vista) or **Printers and Faxes** (Windows XP).

Print Management is included within Administrative Tools in Windows 10, Windows 8, Windows 7, and Windows Vista.

# Recovery Drive

Recovery Drive is a tool used to copy system files to a USB device so that, in the event of a problem, you can repair Windows or reinstall the whole operating system.

It's included in the Windows 10 Administrative Tools only, but you can open it elsewhere in Windows 8. Older versions of Windows have other recovery options, such as the System Repair Disc in Windows 7.

# Registry Editor

Registry Editor is the built-in editor for the Windows Registry.

There's little reason for the average computer user to access this tool, but some deep customizations and troubleshooting does take place through Registry Editor.

Registry Editor is available from Administrative Tools only in Windows 10. However, the tool itself is available in other versions of Windows, too, through the 'regedit' command.

# Reliability and Performance Monitor

Reliability and Performance Monitor is a tool used to monitor statistics about system issues and important hardware in your computer.

It's part of Administrative Tools in Windows Vista. In Windows 10, Windows 8, and Windows 7, the "Performance" features of this tool became **Performance Monitor**, which you can read more about at the bottom of this list.

The "Reliability" features were moved out of Administrative Tools and became part of the Action Center applet in Control Panel.

# Resource Monitor

Resource Monitor is a tool used to view details about current CPU, memory, disk, and network activity that individual processes are utilizing.

It's included in Administrative Tools in Windows 10 and Windows 8. Resource Monitor is also available in Windows 7 and Windows Vista but not via Administrative Tools.

In those older versions of Windows, execute **resmon** to quickly bring it up.

# Services

Services is an MMC snap-in used to manage the various Windows services existing that help your computer start, and then keep running, as you expect.

The Services tool is most often used to change the *startup type* for a particular service, which changes when or how the service is executed. Choices include **Automatic (Delayed Start)**, **Automatic**, **Manual**, and **Disabled**.

This is included within Administrative Tools in Windows 10, Windows 8, Windows 7, Windows Vista, and Windows XP.

# System Configuration

The System Configuration link starts System Configuration, a tool used to help troubleshoot some kinds of Windows startup problems.

It's included within Administrative Tools in Windows 10, Windows 8, Windows 7, and Windows Vista. In Windows 7, the tool can be used to manage the programs that launch when Windows starts up.

It's also available in Windows XP but just not within Administrative Tools. Execute **msconfig** to start it.

# System Information

The System Information link opens the System Information program, a tool that displays incredibly detailed data about the hardware, drivers, and most parts of your computer.

It's included within Administrative Tools in Windows 10 and Windows 8. The System Information tool is included with Windows 7, Windows Vista, and Windows XP as well but just not within Administrative Tools; execute **msinfo32** to start it in those earlier versions of Windows.

Third-party system information programs can also be used to view specific details about your computer.

# Task Scheduler

Task Scheduler is an MMC snap-in used to schedule a task or program to run automatically on a specific date and time.

Some non-Windows programs may use Task Scheduler to set up things like a disk cleanup or defrag tool to run automatically.

It's included within Administrative Tools in Windows 10, Windows 8, Windows 7, and Windows Vista. A task scheduling program, called **Scheduled Tasks**, is also included in Windows XP but is not part of this toolset.

# Windows Firewall With Advanced Security

Windows Firewall with Advanced Security is an MMC snap-in used for advanced configuration of the software firewall included with Windows.

Basic firewall management is best performed via the Windows Firewall applet in Control Panel.

Some versions of windows call this Windows Defender Firewall with Advanced Security.

It's included within Administrative Tools in Windows 10, Windows 8, Windows 7, and Windows Vista.

The firewall built-in to Windows is enabled by default, but you can always disable it and use a third-party program. There are plenty of free firewall programs to pick from.

# Windows Memory Diagnostic

The Windows Memory Diagnostic link starts a scheduling tool for running Windows Memory Diagnostic during the next computer restart.

It tests your computer's memory when Windows isn't running, which is why you can only schedule a memory test and not run one immediately from within Windows.

This is included within Administrative Tools in Windows 10, Windows 8, and Windows 7. This tool is also available in this folder in Windows Vista but is referred to as **Memory Diagnostics Tool**.

There are other free memory testing applications that you can use besides Microsoft's, which we rank and review in our list of free memory test programs.

# Windows PowerShell ISE

Windows PowerShell ISE starts Windows PowerShell Integrated Scripting Environment (ISE), a graphical host environment for PowerShell.

PowerShell is a powerful command-line utility and scripting language that administrators can use to control various aspects of local and remote Windows systems.

Windows PowerShell ISE is included within Administrative Tools in Windows 8. It's also available in Windows 7 and Windows Vista but not via Administrative Tools—those versions of Windows do, however, have a link to a PowerShell command line.

# Windows PowerShell Modules

The Windows PowerShell Modules link starts Windows PowerShell and then automatically executes the *ImportSystemModules* cmdlet.

Windows PowerShell Modules is included within Administrative Tools in Windows 7. You'll also see it as part of Administrative Tools in Windows Vista but only if the optional Windows PowerShell 2.0 is installed.

Windows PowerShell 2.0 can be downloaded for free from Microsoft here as part of the Windows Management Framework Core.